Enjoy the charts!
Chad Daybell

The LDS TOP 5 Charts

The LDS TOP 5 Charts

Where do your favorite LDS celebrities and sports stars rank?

compiled by CHAD DAYBELL

spring creek
BOOK COMPANY

© 2006 Chad Daybell

All Rights Reserved.

This is not an official publication of The Church of Jesus Christ of Latter-day Saints.

ISBN 13: 978-1-932898-56-9
ISBN 10: 1-932898-56-5
e. 1

Published by:
Spring Creek Book Company
P.O. Box 50355
Provo, Utah 84605-0355

www.springcreekbooks.com

Cover design © Spring Creek Book Company
Cover design by Nicole Cunningham

Printed in the United States of America
10 9 8 7 6 5 4 3 2 1
Printed on acid-free paper

Library of Congress Control Number: 2006900362

Table of Contents

Introduction vii
Church Facts 1
   Top 5 U.S. States with the Most LDS Members 2
   Top 5 U.S. States with the Highest Percentage
   of LDS Members.. 3
   Top 5 Countries with the Most LDS Members 4
   Top 5 Countries with the Highest Percentage
   of LDS Members.. 5
   The Longest Tenures of LDS Church Presidents 6

Sports 7
   Top 5 LDS College Football Players 8
   Top 5 LDS Pro Football Players............................. 10
   Top 5 LDS College Basketball Players 12
   Top 5 LDS Pro Basketball Players.......................... 14
   Top 5 LDS Professional Baseball Players 16
   Top 5 LDS Pro Golfers... 18
   Top 5 LDS Olympic Moments 20
   Top 5 BYU Sports Moments 22
   Top 5 BYU Football Teams 24

Entertainment... 27
   Top 5 Biggest Songs by LDS Artists
   on the Billboard Hot 100 28
   Top 5 LDS National Recording Artists 30

Top 5 LDS-based Recording Groups 32
Top 5 LDS-based Male Recording Artists 34
Top 5 LDS-based Female Recording Artists 36
Top 5 LDS Artists/Illustrators 38
Top 5 LDS-based Novelists 40
Top 5 Nationally Published LDS Novelists 42
Top 5 LDS Actors 44
Top 5 LDS Actresses 46
Top 5 LDS-related Television Moments 48
Top 5 LDS Reality TV Celebrities 50
Top 5 LDS-themed Highest-grossing Films 52

Prominent People: Inventors, Businessmen, and Political Leaders 55
Top 5 LDS Inventors 56
Top 5 Best-known LDS Businessmen 58
Top 5 Best-known LDS Political Leaders 60

Bibliography 62
About the Author 63

Introduction

Growing up, I wanted to be either a sports statistician or Casey Kasem's replacement on the *American Top 40* radio countdown. Neither of those jobs quite worked out, merely becoming hobbies of mine. This book, however, is the product of my interest in such things, as well as being a member of the LDS Church.

I need to clarify that to be included in this book, a person doesn't need to be an "active" Mormon. In fact, some of these people weren't even LDS at the time of their greatest accomplishments, but in our humble Mormon way, we have put our arms out and embraced these new converts.

Likewise, if Paul McCartney, Julia Roberts and Shaquille O'Neal all suddenly join the Church, we'll find a place for them in these Top 5 charts.

I have done my best to not include anyone who has openly spoken out against the Church. The people on these charts are comfortable being a Mormon, at least in the cultural sense, and most of them have family members who are active in the Church. One exception is when a person was a member of the Church at the time of his or her historic accomplishment, such as a No. 1 song, and then subsequently left the Church. Those instances are rare, but for now I have included the accomplishment, along with an explanatory note. That policy may change in future editions.

Also, I take sole responsibility for the rankings. Most of the rankings were based on chart positions or sports statistics, but there are a few categories that are as scientific as "Mr. Blackwell's Best Dressed List." I do give credit to Jason Gwilliam and Jon Fernelius for their insightful contributions as we debated the rankings within several of the categories. (On second thought, blame those two guys if you disagree with anything.) I also thank Jack Daybell and Todd Cunningham for their valuable comments and corrections.

This book is simply for entertainment and fun. I have previously written books that contain Church doctrine with eternal significance, but this certainly isn't one of them! The main purpose of this book is to recognize the great accomplishments being made by some very talented members of the Church. An added bonus would be to have you say, "I didn't know that person was LDS," or to introduce you to some entertainment options that you may not have been aware of before reading through the charts.

I give a huge thanks to Ron Johnston and his entertaining website **FamousMormons.net.** Ron's website provided great information and gave me leads of where to look for added details. If you enjoyed this book, you would certainly like reading Ron's new book *Famous Mormons*.

So enjoy the charts! If you happen to question a category's rankings or feel someone has been left out, please e-mail me at the address listed at the back of the book so adjustments can be made in future printings.

Chad Daybell
January 2006

Church Facts

Ever since the Lord told the Church members to keep records, we have done our best to record everything, from tithing amounts to how many people are in sacrament meeting. Here are some other interesting Church-related facts and numbers. They aren't essential to our salvation, but they are fun to know nonetheless.

Top 5 U.S. States with the Most LDS Members

1. Utah (1,720,434 members)
This ranking, determined by information in the *2006 Church Almanac*, should come as no surprise. Utah is still the center of Mormondom, and continues to be a hotbed of missionary work. The largest growth is along the Wasatch Front and in the booming St. George area.

2. California (761,763 members)
The Lord's work is certainly going forward in the Golden State, with 17 different missions and new temples being completed seemingly every year.

3. Idaho (376,661 members)
The state that gave us two consecutive prophets—Ezra Taft Benson and Howard W. Hunter—is definitely holding its own. With BYU-Idaho now a four-year school and with a temple under construction, Rexburg is quickly becoming a major destination for members of the Church.

4. Arizona (346,677 members)
This warm, inviting state has added more than 75,000 members in the last 10 years. It will likely give Idaho some competition in the near future. The strong business climate in Phoenix and Tucson are adding to the Church's growth there.

5. Texas (243,957 members)
This is another state that has had a nice growth spurt in the past 10 years, adding about 60,000 members since 1995.

Honorable Mention
Florida is next at 123,000 Church members, and growing.

Top 5 U.S. States with the Highest Percentage of LDS Members

1. Utah (72 percent)
Although this percentage has dipped compared to previous decades, it can partly be contributed to good non-LDS people moving to Utah because they like the state. LDS parents are still giving their best efforts to outpopulate the newcomers, though.

2. Idaho (27 percent)
Idaho has actually stayed steady at this percentage for the past decade, and still has a sizable lead on any other state.

3. Wyoming (11 percent)
I suppose this proves that maybe only 89 percent of the state's residents hate BYU's sports teams.

4. Nevada (7.1 percent)
This state's percentage has dipped by about a percentage point over the past decade, but with Las Vegas exploding, the state has added nearly a million people in that time. The Church itself grew by more than 40,000 members since 1995.

5. Arizona (6.0 percent)
Arizona's percentage has also remained fairly steady despite an enormous influx of people to the state in recent years.

Honorable Mention
The tropical paradise of **Hawaii** is showing steady growth. Currently, 5.1 percent of the state's residents are Church members, with nearly 10,000 more members than a decade ago.

California remains steady at 2.12 percent.

Top 5 Countries with the Most LDS Members

1. **United States (5,503,192 members)**
   Earlier this decade, the Church reached the milestone of having more members outside of the United States than in it. The United States obviously still has a substantial lead over any other country, however.

2. **Mexico (980,053 members)**
   The figure above is based on the statistics in the *2006 Church Almanac*, but Church leaders estimate that Mexico now has more than a million members. This is an increase of more than 250,000 members in just 10 years, and the pace is quickening.

3. **Brazil (897,091 members)**
   Despite Mexico's amazing growth, it might not be able to hold off Brazil for too long. Ten years ago Brazil had just over a half million members, and has added nearly 400,000 members in that time.

4. **Philippines (537,014 members)**
   The gospel message was first spread by U.S. servicemen stationed there in the 1950s. Soon the Church was growing rapidly throughout the islands and continues to do so.

5. **Chile (534,754 members)**
   Chile now has nearly 80 stakes. The amazing thing is that there were only 20,000 members in the whole country when Elder Gordon B. Hinckley organized its first stake in 1972.

Honorable Mention:
Peru has 402,230 members of the Church and is experiencing the same fascinating growth as other South American nations.

Top 5 Countries with the Highest Percentage of LDS Members

1. Tonga (46 percent)
The growth of the LDS Church in this island nation is truly remarkable. With an estimated population of 115,000 people, nearly 53,000 of them are members of the Church.

2. Samoa (36 percent)
The same phenomenal growth that is taking place in Tonga is happening in Samoa. There are 177,000 residents, and 64,000 of them are members of the Church.

3. Chile (3.3 percent)
Just over 30 years ago, Chile's percentage was essentially zero. When you consider the size of this nation, if it continues to steadily increase its percentage of members, it will add millions of people to the Church.

4. Uruguay (2.5 percent)
This South American country is smaller than some of its neighbors, and so it doesn't have their flashy baptismal numbers, but the missionary work is definitely flourishing there.

5. New Zealand (2.35 percent)
The gospel was first well-received by the Maori people, but in recent years the citizens of European ancestry have also been joining the Church in large numbers.

Honorable mention:
In the United States, 1.9 percent of the citizens are members of the Church. That might sound small, but that is 1 in 50 Americans. The pioneers could never have imagined it.

The 5 Longest Tenures of LDS Church Presidents

1. **Brigham Young (33 years)**
   The second president of the LDS Church valiantly carried the burdens of the Church through the hard times after Joseph Smith's death. He established Salt Lake City and saw dozens of other Mormon settlements spread across the West.

2. **Heber J. Grant (26 years)**
   When Joseph F. Smith passed away in 1918, Heber J. Grant became the president at the relatively young age of 62. His presidency spanned many notable events—the aftermath of World War I, the Roaring Twenties, and the Great Depression. He died just before the official end of World War II.

3. **David O. McKay (19 years)**
   He began his presidency in 1951 and presided over a great period of growth in the Church. When he passed away in 1970, he was the only prophet many members had ever known.

4. **Joseph F. Smith (17 years)**
   The son of Hyrum Smith saw the Church progress from the days of covered wagons in Nauvoo to airplanes in Salt Lake City. His wisdom guided the Church through the early 20th Century.

5. **Joseph Smith (14 years)**
   His presidency began with the establishment of the Church in 1830 and laid the foundation for the gospel to spread across the world. No mortal man has accomplished greater things.

Honorable Mention
   At the end of 2005, **Gordon B. Hinckley** had served as president for more than 10 years and was still going strong at age 95.

Sports

The LDS world is filled with great athletes. Starting with Joseph Smith, who could easily win any stick-pulling contest or throw the local bully into a ditch. Maybe it is because of those rough-and-tumble beginnings, but football and wrestling are certainly sports where LDS athletes excel. Members of the Church have competed with the world's best athletes in a variety of sports, and they have often returned home victorious.

Top 5 LDS College Football Players

1. **Ty Detmer, BYU**
   Ty didn't have the prototype quarterback body, but he sure could win games and throw the football. Ty still holds dozens of NCAA passing records. His amazing record of 15,031 career passing yards stood until 2004. His efforts were rewarded with several top honors, including the 1990 Heisman Trophy. His career began as a freshman in the 1988 Freedom Bowl, with his best on-the-field moment being the victory over No. 1-ranked Miami. He was named first-team All-American in both 1990 and 1991, and he won the Davey O'Brien Award as the top college quarterback those same years. Ty joined the LDS Church while he attended BYU.

2. **Scott Mitchell, Utah**
   Until Scott's arrival on campus, the University of Utah football team never had such a prolific passer. Scott made the most of coach Jim Fassel's wide-open offense to compile some amazing stats. Scott averaged an astounding 392 passing yards per game in 1988, which included 631 yards against Air Force. His highlight that season was the 57-28 blowout of BYU, ending a 10-year losing streak against the Cougars.

3. **Luke Staley, BYU**
   Few players created the excitement that Luke did each time he took a handoff. Luke led the nation in 2001 with 15.5 points per game and 8.1 yards per carry. He set BYU single-season records of 28 touchdowns and 1,582 yards rushing on the season. He was BYU's first consensus All-American since 1991. Luke was drafted by the Detroit Lions and had success in some pre-season games, but injuries ended his promising NFL career.

4. Robbie Bosco, BYU

In his two years as a starter for the Cougars, Robbie compiled a 24-3 record, threw for 8,148 yards., and tossed 66 touchdown passes. The crowning performance of Robbie's career came in the 1984 Holiday Bowl when he led two fourth-quarter touchdown drives that completed their 13-0 season and locked up the national championship. Robbie was a consensus All-American both seasons, and finished third in the Heisman Trophy in both 1984 and 1985. The three losses during his career were by a total of 13 points. Robbie was Green Bay's third-round draft pick and played two years for the Packers before his NFL career was shortened by a shoulder injury.

5. Steve Young, BYU

Although some would expect Steve to rank higher in this category, this is a fair representation of his college career. He climbed from the eighth spot on BYU's depth chart to earn the starting job in 1982. His most memorable moment came in the 1983 Holiday Bowl when he caught a halfback pass and scored the winning touchdown against Missouri. The Cougars finished the season 11-1. Steve was named WAC Player of the Year in 1983 and was a consensus All-American. He finished second in the 1983 Heisman Trophy voting behind Nebraska running back Mike Rozier.

Honorable "potential"

Ben Olson has yet to even play in a college game, yet the former high school All-American and 2002's ESPN National Player of the Year has the potential to become a star as UCLA's quarterback. After a redshirt year at BYU, a two-year mission to Canada, and then a year on the sidelines for UCLA, his time has finally come. With his size and skills, along with a talented team, Ben could quickly climb into the Top 5 of this category. He very likely has an NFL career ahead of him.

Top 5 LDS Pro Football Players

1. **Steve Young**
   Steve's professional career started a little rocky, playing two seasons with the ill-fated USFL's Los Angeles Express, followed by another two years with the Tampa Bay Buccaneers. He then joined the San Francisco 49ers in 1987 and watched Hall of Famer Joe Montana lead the team for four years. But when Steve finally got his chance as the starter, he made the most of it. He was voted NFL Most Valuable Player in 1992 and 1994 and was runner-up in 1993. Steve led the 49ers to a victory over the San Diego Chargers in Super Bowl XXIX, throwing a record six touchdown passes on his way to being named the game's MVP. He also won six NFL passing titles during his career and is known as one of the most accurate passers in NFL history. What made Steve different from most quarterbacks was his constant threat as a runner. He ran for 4,239 yards and scored 43 rushing touchdowns in his NFL career. He was elected to the NFL Hall of Fame in 2005. Steve earned his law degree from BYU and also works as a TV football analyst.

2. **Merlin Olsen**
   Merlin was a big yet agile defensive tackle for the Los Angeles Rams from 1962-1976. He was a first-round draft pick after an All-American career at Utah State University, and he continued to improve in the NFL, winning Rookie of the Year honors. Merlin led the Rams' "Fearsome Foursome" defensive line and was named All-NFL several times while going to the Pro Bowl 14 consecutive years. He was elected to the NFL Hall of Fame in 1982. Merlin went on to have a successful television career as an actor on the TV shows *Little House on the Prairie* and *Father Murphy*, as well as doing commentary for NFL games.

3. Todd Christensen

Todd was an above-average running back for the BYU Cougars who could also catch passes. As a pro, he joined the Los Angeles Raiders, converted to tight end, and became a star. Todd led the NFL in receptions in 1983 with 92 catches. He led the Raiders in receptions from 1982 to 1986, and he was an All-Pro pick each of those seasons. Todd was a member of the 1981 Raiders squad that defeated the Philadelphia Eagles in Super Bowl XV, and he led the Raiders to another Super Bowl victory in 1983. He remains close to the game, working as a football analyst for network television.

4. Danny White

Danny was the starting quarterback for the Dallas Cowboys in the 1980s and led the team to three straight NFC title games. He set several team passing records, and his record as a starter was 67-35. Danny is now the head coach and general manager of the Utah Blaze in the Arena Football League.

5. Scott Mitchell

After being drafted by the Miami Dolphins and making a strong impression while filling in for an injured Dan Marino, Scott signed with the Detroit Lions and was their starter for several seasons. In 1995, Scott combined with Hall of Fame running back Barry Sanders to create an explosive offense. That season Scott threw for 4,338 yards and 32 touchdowns, including 410 passing yards in a Thanksgiving Day win over the Vikings.

Honorable mention

This is easily the toughest category to narrow down. Gifford Nielsen, Merrill Hodge, Marc Wilson, Bart Oates, Jason Buck, Via Sikahema, Eric Hipple, Ty Detmer, Chad Lewis, Kevin Curtis, Todd Heap, Doug Jolley, John Tait, Ryan Denney and many other LDS players have had successful NFL careers.

Top 5 LDS College Basketball Players

1. **Danny Ainge, BYU**
   Danny's first three years at BYU were certainly memorable, but he truly solidified his spot at the top of this list when he led the Cougars to the Elite Eight in the NCAA Tournament in 1981. His shot to beat Notre Dame in the last seconds is an all-time highlight. That year he averaged 24.4 points per game and led the Cougars to a 25-7 record. He made essentially every All-American team while winning the Eastman and John Wooden awards as college basketball's player of the year. His 2,467 career points still rank as the most by a Cougar, and he set an NCAA record by scoring in double figures in 112 straight games. Danny was gifted in many sports and would play professional baseball with the Toronto Blue Jays in the summers during college. Finally, after his stellar senior season, the Boston Celtics drafted him and bought out his baseball contract.

2. **Devin Durrant, BYU**
   Cougar basketball fans sometimes forget how blessed they were in the early 1980s. As Danny Ainge's college career was winding down, Devin's career was just beginning. The two actually both started for the 1979-80 team before Devin went on a two-year mission to Spain. Devin started every game of his BYU career, and after his return from Spain, he led the Cougars to two WAC championships and two NCAA Tournament berths. During Devin's senior year he averaged more than 30 points a game and scored 866 points, a BYU record. He finished with 2,285 career points. Devin earned many honors after his senior season, including being named a consensus All-American. He later played in the NBA for the Indiana Pacers and Phoenix Suns, and he is now a successful businessman and author.

3. Casey Jacobsen, Stanford

Casey led Stanford to national prominence in 2001 and 2002. He was selected as a first-team All-American as a sophomore, when he averaged 18 points per game and made 47 percent of his three-point shots. He ranks third on Stanford's career scoring list with 1,723 points. Casey was chosen by the Phoenix Suns in the first round in the 2002 NBA draft. He now plays for the New Orleans Hornets.

4. Tom Chambers, Utah

Tom's college career wasn't quite as flashy as his NBA career turned out to be, but there were signs of brilliance, and he and teammate Danny Vranes were a constant thorn in the side of BYU and the rest of the WAC. Tom was chosen in the first round of the 1981 NBA draft by the San Diego Clippers.

5. Kresimir Cosic, BYU

The tall, strong center from Yugoslavia entertained fans with his constant enthusiasm for the game. At BYU, Kresimir was named All-Conference three times and was named an All-American his senior year after averaging 20.2 points per game. Kresimir then played for and helped coach the Yugoslavian Olympic team, winning a gold medal in 1980. Kresimir passed away in 1995.

Honorable mention

Michael Smith was the leader of the 1987-88 BYU team that started 17-0 and was ranked as high as No. 2 in the nation. His "California cool" flat-top and smooth shooting made him a fan favorite. He was drafted in the first round by the Boston Celtics. He is now a TV and radio analyst for the L.A. Clippers.

Shawn Bradley had a terrific freshman season at BYU, then departed on a mission to Australia. He returned home and was chosen by the 76ers as the No. 2 pick in the NBA draft.

Top 5 LDS Pro Basketball Players

1. **Tom Chambers**
   After a strong college career at the University of Utah, Tom became a scoring machine in the NBA. He was named to four NBA All-Star teams and was named MVP of the 1987 All-Star Game, after scoring 34 points. He was named to the All-NBA Second Team in 1989 and 1990. He combined with All-Star guard Kevin Johnson in an up-tempo offense that kept opponents always on the run. His single-game highlight came when he scored 60 points against the Seattle Supersonics in 1990. Tom averaged more than 20 points per game in five different seasons, topped by a 27.2 average during the 1989-1990 season. His career total of 20,049 points currently ranks him at No. 29 all-time in NBA history. His jersey has been retired by the Phoenix Suns. He spent two seasons at the end of his career with the Utah Jazz in the city where he was a college star.

2. **Danny Ainge**
   After winning nearly every major award after his senior year at BYU, Danny joined the Boston Celtics and helped restore that dynasty to glory. He became teammates with the legendary Larry Bird, and Danny was a starting guard as the Celtics won the NBA championship in 1984 and 1986. Danny was known for his hustling, aggressive play and solid outside shooting. He later played with the Sacramento Kings, Portland Trail Blazers, and Phoenix Suns, retiring in 1994. He became the second player in NBA history to hit 900 three-point shots and the fourth to reach 1,000. He averaged 11.9 points during his NBA career. In 2003 he returned to the Celtics as their executive director of basketball operations, and he has the Celtics on the upswing once again.

3. Natalie Williams

Natalie is currently a member of the Indiana Fever of the WNBA. She is the leading rebounder in U.S. women's professional basketball history, and is the second-leading scorer ever. She was named an All-WNBA First Team selection three straight years and was the leader of the U.S. women's basketball team that captured the gold medal at the 2000 Summer Olympics. She was raised in Taylorsville, Utah, and was honored as Utah's Female Athlete of the 20th Century.

4. Kiki Vandeweghe

Kiki first made a name for himself in the NBA with the Denver Nuggets, where he was selected to the NBA Western Conference All-Star team in 1983 and 1984. He was then traded to the Portland Trail Blazers, where he had several strong seasons. Kiki's career average was an impressive 19.7 points per game.

5. Shawn Bradley

Shawn had a lengthy NBA career, spending the last several seasons with the Dallas Mavericks. He was a solid scorer and rebounder, but he was best-known for his shot-blocking ability. At 7-foot 6-inches tall with a matching wingspan, he altered the shots of many NBA stars. Shawn retired in 2005 with a total of 2,119 blocked shots, ranking tenth all-time in NBA history.

Honorable mention

Thurl Bailey was a key part of the Utah Jazz teams of the late 1980s and early 1990s that were among the best in the NBA. Thurl joined the Church in 1995. He has released a few music CDs and it is safe to say he is the best singer in this category.

Mark "Mad Dog" Madsen won two NBA titles as a member of the Los Angeles Lakers. He was Shaquille O'Neal's backup and helped keep the Lakers in games with his tenacious defense.

Top 5 LDS Professional Baseball Players

1. **Harmon Killebrew**
   So far, Harmon Killebrew is the only LDS member to be inducted into the Baseball Hall of Fame. From 1954-1975 he played a variety of fielding positions for the Washington Senators, Minnesota Twins, and Kansas City Royals. He was best-known for his monstrous home runs. Harmon hit 40 or more homers in eight different seasons, and ended his career with a total of 573. Even after the steroid-fueled home run totals of recent years, Harmon still ranks No. 8 all-time, ahead of such sluggers as Reggie Jackson and Mike Schmidt. His best seasons were with the Twins, where he led the team to the 1965 World Series against the L.A. Dodgers, falling one game short of the title. He later won the American League MVP Award in 1969.

2. **Dale Murphy**
   This true superstar played in the major leagues from 1976 to 1993, primarily with the Atlanta Braves. During his career he hit 398 home runs and accumulated 2,111 hits. He had 100 or more RBIs in five different seasons. He won back-to-back National League MVP awards in 1983 and 1984, and was a seven-time All-Star. He later played with the Philadephia Phillies and Colorado Rockies before his career was shortened by persistent injuries. Most Hall of Fame voters say his career statistics fall just short of induction into the Hall, but they all agree that if a player could be inducted solely based on his example and integrity, Dale would be a unanimous selection for the way he treated others throughout his career. Since his playing days, Dale has served as the president of the Massachusetts Boston Mission from 1997-2000 and continues to serve in the Church and the community.

3. Vernon Law

Vernon pitched in the major leagues from 1950 to 1967. He won 10 or more games in nine different seasons and finished with a career ERA of 3.77. He won the 1960 Cy Young Award with a 20-9 record, and more importantly, was the Pirates' driving force as they won the National League pennant and went on to defeat the heavily favored New York Yankees in the World Series.

4. Jeff Kent

Jeff is still going strong heading into the 2006 season as the second baseman for the Los Angeles Dodgers. As his career progresses, he is even being mentioned as a potential Hall of Famer. He won the National League MVP in 2000 as a member of the San Francisco Giants. He is a five-time All-Star and his career total of 331 home runs are the most ever by a second baseman, surpassing Hall of Famer Ryne Sandberg in 2004.

5. Wally Joyner

Wally is a product of BYU's baseball program in the early 1980s. He played in the major leagues from 1986-2001. He was a true "rookie sensation" for the California Angels, becoming the first rookie to ever be voted to the American League All-Star team. Wally finished his career with a .289 batting average, 204 homers and 1,106 RBIs. Wally now lives in Utah and has had roles in such LDS-themed movies as *The R.M.* and *The Home Teachers*.

Honorable mention

Bruce Hurst pitched for the Boston Red Sox and the San Diego Padres. His career highlight was his stellar performance in the 1986 World Series. Bruce was initially voted the World Series MVP before the New York Mets stormed back to win the title.

Cory Snyder was a feared slugger at BYU before starring for many years with the Cleveland Indians and the L.A. Dodgers.

Top 5 LDS Pro Golfers

1. Billy Casper

Billy emerged in the late 1950s as one of the greatest golfers in the world. During his career he compiled an amazing 51 PGA Tour victories, and he has added another nine titles on the Champions Tour. His accuracy is shown in the fact he made 21 holes-in-one during his pro career. He was the PGA Player of the Year in 1966 and 1970, and he was the U.S. Open champion in 1959 and 1966. The 1966 victory was an all-time classic as he rallied from seven strokes down with nine holes to play to tie Arnold Palmer before winning the ensuing 18-hole playoff. Billy won the Masters Championship in 1970, and he was the second player in history to reach $1 million in earnings, preceded only by Arnold Palmer. Billy was a member of the U.S. Ryder Cup team many times, and he was inducted into the World Golf Hall of Fame in 1978 and the PGA Hall of Fame in 1982. Billy is now retired from pro events, but he has left a memorable legacy.

2. Johnny Miller

After a stellar collegiate career at BYU, Johnny played on the PGA Tour from 1969 to 1994 and won 24 titles. His biggest victory came when he won the 1973 U.S. Open by shooting 63 in the final round, the lowest score ever by an Open winner. He was the PGA Tour's leading money-winner in 1974. He had eight victories that season, and was deservedly named the 1974 PGA Player of the Year. In 1996, Johnny was elected to the PGA Tour Hall of Fame. Johnny now works primarily as the lead analyst for NBC Sports' professional golf telecasts, where he is renowned for his knowledge of the game and for the keen insights he gives to TV viewers. He does occasionally play in charity tournaments with his sons, who are talented golfers in their own right.

3. Mike Reid

Mike is a two-time PGA Tour winner and had a notable career. He now plays on the Champions Tour, where he is having great success. During 2005 he once had a string of 15 successive par-or-better rounds. His season was capped off by his victory at the 2005 Senior PGA Championship. Mike played golf at BYU, graduating in 1976.

4. Dan Forsman

Dan's professional career started in 1992 after he was twice named an All-American at Arizona State. Dan has won five PGA tournaments during his career, most recently in 2002. He was the winner of the 1987 MCI Long Distance Driving Competition.

5. Keith Clearwater

Keith earned two victories on the PGA Tour, both during his rookie season in 1987. His win at the Colonial National Invitational was one of the most unusual in tour history, because he recorded a pair of 64s on a 36-hole final day. He was named the 1987 PGA Tour Rookie of the Year. He was a member of the BYU golf team that won the 1981 NCAA Championship.

Honorable Mention

Jay Don Blake has played on the PGA Tour since 1981 with several strong finishes over the years. He has one tour victory.

Bruce Summerhays has three career wins on the Champions Tour, most recently at the 2004 Kroger Classic.

Author's note: After winning the Masters Championship in 2003, it was widely reported that **Mike Weir** was Mormon. Although his wife is LDS and they reside in Utah, Mike is not a member of the LDS Church.

Top 5 LDS Olympic Moments

1. **Rulon Gardner, 2000 gold medal wrestler**
   Rulon pulled off the biggest upset of the 2000 Summer Olympics when he defeated Russian superstar Alexander Karelin in the Greco-Roman wrestling final. Karelin had been undefeated for 13 years, and had not given up a point in six years. After the 2000 Olympics, Rulon suffered a series of injuries, including an amputated toe and a dislocated wrist. He was also in a motorcycle accident. Despite his injuries, he won the U.S. Olympic trials for his weight class and competed in the 2004 Summer Olympics, winning the bronze medal. After the bronze medal match, he left his shoes on the mat as a traditional symbol of retirement.

2. **Peter Vidmar, 1984 gold medal gymnast**
   Peter was the smiling young man who led the United States men's gymnastics team to unprecedented heights at the 1984 Summer Olympics. Peter was the team captain, and he certainly performed like it, leading the team to its first-ever gold medal. He also captured the individual gold medal on the pommel horse by scoring a perfect 10. He also won a silver medal in the individual all-around men's competition. His winning combined scores averaged 9.89, making him the highest-scoring U.S. male gymnast in Olympic history.

3. **Cael Sanderson, 2004 gold medal wrestler**
   Cael won the 185-pound freestyle wrestling gold medal at the 2004 Summer Olympics, despite facing the tremendous pressure of being a favorite after his outstanding college career at Iowa State University in which he finished a perfect 159-0 and won four NCAA titles. Cael certainly came through in the clutch at the Olympics. He trailed by one point entering the final round of the gold medal match, but with 54 seconds remaining, he completed a takedown to win the coveted gold medal.

4. Mark Schultz, 1984 gold medal wrestler

Mark's wrestling accomplishments are as long as this page, with significant victories at every level. His most memorable win, though, came when he won a gold medal for the United States at the 1984 Summer Olympics. The moment was even more special when his brother Dave also won a wrestling gold medal. Together, Mark and Dave were the first American brothers to each win gold medals in the same Olympics, and likewise the first to win World and Olympic championships. A highlight after their victories was a visit with U.S. President Ronald Reagan, who congratulated the brothers on their accomplishments. Mark later coached BYU's wrestling team for many years.

5. Alma Richards, 1912 gold medal, track & field

Alma was a native of Parowan, Utah, and he became the first Utahn to win an Olympic gold medal at Stockholm, Sweden, in 1912. He beat teammate Jim Thorpe, the proclaimed "world's greatest athlete," to claim his high jump gold medal at a height of 6 feet 4 inches. The mark set a new world record. Alma received his gold medal from King Gustav of Sweden, who jokingly asked him how he managed to jump so high. Alma was a BYU student at the time, and Provo's citizens held a huge celebration in his honor at the city's train station when he returned home.

Honorable mention:

Rowdy Gaines became a household name as a swimmer for the United States during the 1984 Olympic Summer Games. He won three gold medals and broke two world records. He was baptized a member of the Church in Birmingham, Alabama, in 1998.

Laura Berg was a member of the United States women's softball teams that won gold medals in 1996 and 2000. In the 2000 games she was the team's starting centerfielder and her timely hitting and fielding played a big part in the team's victories.

Top 5 BYU Sports Moments

1. **1984 football national championship**
   After twelve games in 1984, the Cougars were unbeaten and ranked No. 1 in the country. But in the third quarter of the 1984 Holiday Bowl, things were admittedly looking a little bleak. BYU fans truly hoped backup quarterback Blaine Fowler would be able to lead a Cougar comeback, but when star quarterback Robbie Bosco courageously hobbled back onto the field after being sidelined by an injured ankle, faith was restored. Two Bosco touchdown passes later, BYU was the national champion.

2. **1980 Holiday Bowl**
   This is the game that every true Cougar fan claims to have watched until the very end, but realistically most fans went to bed once BYU fell behind the SMU Mustangs by the score of 45-25 with four minutes left in the game. But miracles do happen, and quarterback Jim McMahon carried the team those final minutes, capping things off with a touchdown bomb to tight end Clay Brown on the final play that tied the score. Kurt Gunther kicked the extra point, and the Cougars pulled off a stunning 46-45 victory that left even LaVell Edwards smiling.

3. **Danny Ainge's winning shot against Notre Dame**
   In 1981, the BYU men's basketball team began an amazing run through the NCAA Tournament. The Cougars opened with easy victories over Princeton and UCLA, landing them in the Sweet Sixteen. Next up was powerful Notre Dame. It was a tough battle, and with eight seconds left, BYU trailed by one point. Danny Ainge took the inbounds pass and dribbled through three defenders at mid-court. Then he slipped past the other two defenders and made a twisting lay-up at the buzzer, giving BYU a 51-50 win and a berth in the Elite Eight. BYU lost their next game to No. 1 Virginia, but Danny's shot will live on.

4. Ty Detmer winning the Heisman Trophy

In 1990, Ty Detmer's spectacular junior season made him the front-runner for the Heisman Trophy as college football's best player. But would the Heisman voters give it to a player from the Mountain West? It was definitely the most interesting Heisman Trophy presentation in history, as Ty sat with Coach LaVell Edwards and the rest of the BYU team in front of a TV camera in sunny Hawaii while the other Heisman candidates were in New York City. The spontaneous celebration that occurred when Ty's name was announced was unforgettable, and was almost as unlikely as BYU winning the 1984 national title. Cougar fans would rather forget that night's game against Hawaii, as well as the Holiday Bowl against Texas A&M, but they'll never forget the day Ty was crowned the best player in the land.

5. Beating No. 1 Miami in 1990

The key game that led to Ty Detmer's eventual Heisman Trophy win took place in the second game of the season against the Miami Hurricanes, the nation's No. 1 team. In front of a national TV audience, BYU dismantled Miami. Ty had a big game, both statistically and emotionally. He was fired up, and the rest of the team followed his lead—as did most of the fans in Cougar Stadium. The Cougars held on for a 28-21 victory, which launched them back into the national spotlight.

Honorable mention

Steve Young's touchdown catch in the final seconds to beat Missouri 24-21 in the 1983 Holiday Bowl—and his subsequent high-stepping victory dance in the endzone—capped an 11-1 season and cemented Steve's place in BYU history.

Luke Staley's stunning last-minute touchdown run down the sideline against Utah in 2001 kept BYU undefeated at 11-0. Too bad it all unraveled two weeks later.

Top 5 BYU Football Teams

1. 1984 (13-0 record)
For years, BYU had come so close to a perfect season, but there always seemed to be an opening-game defeat or a Holiday Bowl loss that would leave a sour taste. Robbie Bosco made sure neither one of those things was going to happen. The Cougars jumped right out of the gate by upsetting No. 3 Pittsburgh. This propelled BYU into the national rankings. There were close calls against Hawaii and Utah State, but otherwise the Cougars sailed along, watching the national powerhouses lose games. At the end of the regular season, BYU was the only undefeated major college team and ranked No. 1. Their victory over Michigan in the Holiday Bowl locked up the national title.

2. 1980 (12-1 record)
Ahh, the Jim McMahon era, when the quarterback's cockiness began to rub off on the fans. Beating UTEP 83-7 just didn't feel like a big enough win, did it? Only an unfathomable 25-21 loss at New Mexico to open the season marred the accomplishments of this outstanding team. Of course, the year was capped off with the unforgettable 46-45 Miracle Bowl win against SMU.

3. 1996 (14-1 record)
The only blemish on the season was a 29-17 loss to a powerful Washington team in Seattle. They basically slaughtered most opponents, scoring at least 30 points in 10 games. The capstone of the season was a comeback victory against Kansas State in the Cotton Bowl on New Year's Day 1997. The Cougars were down 15-5 at one point, but they rallied to take an exciting 19-15 victory. They finished ranked in the Top 5 of the polls. Steve Sarkesian is easily the most underated BYU quarterback ever, but he has proven his football smarts at USC as the quarterbacks coach for 2004 Heisman Trophy winner Matt Leinhart.

4. 1983 (11-1 record)

Let's face it, after the 1982 season ended with an 8-4 record and a devastating 47-17 loss to Ohio State in the Holiday Bowl, most Cougar fans weren't too keen on that descendant of Brigham Young who was quarterbacking the team. The mood of Cougar Nation got even more surly after the 1983 season opened with a loss at Baylor. But eleven consecutive wins later, BYU fans were ready to embrace Steve Young with open arms as he moved on to the riches of the ... USFL. Thankfully, we know the story has a happy ending.

5. 1979 (11-1 record)

Remember Marc Wilson? He was the Cougar quarterback—and bonafide hero—for 11 games in 1979. He is deservedly listed among the best players to come out of the Quarterback Factory, sandwiched right there between Gifford Nielsen and Jim McMahon. But he came one agonizing point away from immortality. The Cougars had an 11-0 record heading into the Holiday Bowl, where they let a less-talented 7-4 Indiana team steal a 38-37 victory. BYU outplayed the Hoosiers all night, but they missed a short field goal with seven seconds remaining that would have won the game. Sadly, the 1979 team is overlooked when the great BYU teams are mentioned. The biggest travesty of all is that Indiana's coach at the time, Lee Corso, is now a national TV sports commentator and he just can't help bringing up that game every chance he gets.

Honorable mention

2001 (12-2 record). Running back Luke Staley, quarterback Brandon Doman, and first-year coach Gary Crowton looked amazing during their 12-0 start. If Luke hadn't broken his ankle against Mississippi State, this season might have ended differently. Luke still earned several honors as the nation's top running back with 1,596 rushing yards and 28 touchdowns.

Entertainment

Members of the LDS Church have had a strong positive impact on the entertainment world. From music to film to art, Church members are finding success on both the LDS and international stages. You may have heard of most of the people who are on the following charts, but most likely some of them will make you say, "Wow! I didn't know that person was a Mormon!" Enjoy this LDS-based journey into the entertainment world.

Top 5 Biggest Songs by LDS Artists on the Billboard Hot 100

1. **"One Bad Apple" by The Osmonds**

    The Osmonds had been in the national consciousness for several years, having appeared regularly on "The Andy Williams Show" and on Jerry Lewis' variety show, but had yet to have a hit record. That all changed in 1971, as their song "One Bad Apple" quickly rushed to the No. 1 spot in six weeks, and then spent another five weeks at the top. Suddenly, young women across the world had a new set of teen music idols to admire. The fan frenzy known as "Osmondmania" ruled for the next three years, and the fans in England were even more rabid than in America, if possible. The group had 11 different million-selling records in one year, which set a standard that is still unmatched. It all started with this catchy little pop song.

2. **"Go Away, Little Girl" by Donny Osmond**

    As the Osmond machine began to pick up steam in 1971, the decision was made by the group's producer to have Donny record solo. He was the reigning cover boy at the time on all of the teen magazines, Donny recorded a cover version of "Go Away, Little Girl," which had gone to No. 1 for Steve Lawrence in 1963. Donny's version also became a smash, spending three weeks at the top of the chart. It became the first song in the rock era to be No. 1 by two different artists. Donny then charted with several other songs, including "Puppy Love" which climbed to No. 3. In 1989, Donny returned to the airwaves with "Soldier of Love." The song took off and went all the way to No. 2. The song helped restart his music career, and he continues to record CDs and give concerts. He also performed for many years as Joseph in the stage production of *Joseph and the Technicolor Dreamcoat*.

3. "American Woman" by The Guess Who

This one likely came as a shocker, but Canadian rock star and LDS convert Randy Bachman wrote and performed this classic. It spent three weeks at No. 1 in 1970 and has since been remade many times, including by Randy himself. The song was recently a big hit once again, this time for Lenny Kravitz.

4. "Midnight Train to Georgia" by Gladys Knight

This song spent two weeks at No. 1 in 1973 and is considered one of the classic songs of all-time. Gladys was also credited with a No. 1 song as a featured artist on Dionne Warwick's song, "That's What Friends Are For." Gladys and Dionne were joined on that song by music legends Stevie Wonder and Elton John. The song stayed at No. 1 for four weeks in 1985.

5. "You Ain't Seen Nothin' Yet" by Bachman-Turner Overdrive

After joining the Church, Randy Bachman didn't like the lifestyle that surrounded The Guess Who, so he left the band and started his own with two of his brothers and a friend. Randy was soon back to creating big hits, taking this song all the way to No. 1 for one week in 1974. Randy is no longer a member of the Church.

Honorable Mention

The Jets, composed of members of the Wolfgramm family, had five Top 10 singles from 1986-1988, including two No. 3 hits, "Crush on You" and "You Got It All." The song "Make It Real" went to No. 4.

Author's note: **Christina Aguilera**'s parents attended BYU and were married in the Washington D.C. Temple, but they divorced when Christina was young and there is no evidence she was ever baptized into the LDS Church. She has had four No. 1 songs and several Top 5 hits so far in her career.

Top 5 LDS National Recording Artists

1. **The Osmond Family**

    The members of this family could fill up several of these slots, but we'll combine them into one entry. Alan, Wayne, Merrill, Jay, and Donny sang five-part harmony as The Osmonds, emerging as true superstars in the early 1970s. Some of their many hits included, "One Bad Apple," "Double Lovin'," "Yo Yo," "Down By The Lazy River," and "Crazy Horses." The group officially disbanded in 1980, but then the older four members of the group later reunited and performed as a country act for several years. Donny and Marie recorded albums together and performed each week throughout the late 1970s on the popular TV variety program *The Donny & Marie Show*. Both Donny and Marie each had several big solo hits. Even youngest brother Jimmy got into the act with a No. 1 single in the United Kingdom.

2. **Gladys Knight**

    Gladys Knight & the Pips have been a fixture of the American music scene since the 1960s. The group, which consisted of Gladys and her backup-singing cousins, had 26 hits on the Top 40, including "Midnight Train to Georgia" and "I Heard It Through the Grapevine." Gladys was baptized into the LS Church in August 1997. In 2000, she produced her first inspirational album, *Many Different Roads*, and in 2002, she organized a choir "to provide an opportunity for people who wouldn't come otherwise to an LDS meeting, where they will hear a strong Christ-centered message of the restored gospel." The choir consists of more than 100 members from the greater Las Vegas area, and they bring a new level of passion to the traditionally reserved LDS hymns. Gladys Knight & the Pips were inducted into the Rock and Roll Hall of Fame in 1996.

ENTERTAINMENT   31

3. SHe-DAISY

The Osborne sisters—Kristyn, Kelsi and Kassidy—grew up in Magna, Utah, and have released several hit CDs. (The group's name comes from a Native American word meaning "my sisters.") Their biggest success has been on the country singles chart. They broke onto the charts with the single "Little Good-Byes." Since then they have had a steady stream of Top 10 hits, with several songs crossing over to the pop charts. This trend is expected to continue when they release their new CD in early 2006.

4. The Jets

In the late 1980s, few groups had as many hits as The Jets. The group was composed of members of the Wolfgramm family who left their native Tonga in 1965 for Minneapolis, Minnesota. The Jets dominated the airwaves with catchy dance singles like "Crush on You" and ballads such as "You Got It All." The group reunited in 1997 for the gospel-oriented CD *Love Will Find the Way*.

5. Brandon Flowers

Brandon is the lead singer and keyboardist of The Killers, a rock group from Las Vegas. *SPIN Magazine* called them the hottest band of 2005. They have played a series of sold-out concerts over the past two years. Their debut CD *Hot Fuss* is a multi-platinum success all over the world. It includes the hits "Somebody Told Me" and "Mr. Brightside." The group's new CD, due in early summer of 2006, could propel Brandon to superstardom.

Honorable mention

Dan Truman plays keyboard for Diamond Rio, a country group with several big hits. Dan studied classical piano at BYU.

Author's note: **Randy Bachman** was the main songwriter of The Guess Who and Bachman-Turner Overdrive. He converted to the Church and was a member for several years, but he is no longer a member, nor is his son, musician Tal Bachman.

Top 5 LDS-based Recording Groups

1. **Mormon Tabernacle Choir**
   It might seem too obvious to list the Mormon Tabernacle Choir on a page of famous Mormon musicians. On the other hand, with a Grammy Award and four Gold Records, they truly belong here. Their weekly program "Music and the Spoken Word" was first broadcast in 1929, and has been going strong ever since. The choir is made up of 360 volunteers who range in age from 25 to 60. They are accompanied by a volunteer orchestra of 110 musicians. President Ronald Reagan labeled the Mormon Tabernacle Choir as "America's Choir," and at his 1989 inauguration, President George Bush proclaimed it "a national treasure. Their many albums have sold millions of copies to LDS and non-LDS fans alike. They even made the Billboard Top 40 in 1959, climbing to No. 13 with their rendition of "The Battle Hymn of the Republic." There is a good chance they'll keep on performing until the Second Coming—and beyond.

2. **Afterglow**
   Afterglow is the best known and the best-selling musical duo in LDS music history. Joel McCausland and Kevin Peay began their musical career together in Pleasant Grove, Utah. As juniors in high school they would perform for community groups and at LDS firesides. After their LDS missions, the duo signed a recording contract with Deseret Book. They have since recorded nearly 20 albums for the label, and their smooth harmonies and inspiring lyrics have been favorites for more than 25 years. Their "greatest hits" albums are among the best-selling LDS-based CDs of all-time and their fanbase in some families now spans three generations. They have also recorded country albums as McCoslyn & Paye (slightly tweaking their last names).

ENTERTAINMENT

3. Jericho Road

As the music tastes of the teen generation turned to more of a hip-hop sound, these four talented singers in this group filled the void in the LDS market. Their songs are a solid mix of ballads and upbeat, danceable tunes that are similar to what is found in the national market. The welcome difference is Jericho Road's profanity-free, non-suggestive lyrics. The group sold 100,000 CDs in less than two years, and their third album *There Is More* was released in 2005 and is racking up similar numbers.

4. Ryan Shupe & the Rubberband

This group has been an underground sensation for a few years in the LDS market, but they reached the big time with their latest CD *Dream Big*. Both the CD and the title track climbed the country charts. The song plays over the opening credits of the NBC television series *Three Wishes* starring Amy Grant.

5. The 5 Browns

This youthful quintet of piano-playing brothers and sisters love classical music and were trained at New York's Juilliard School. Their debut CD has received a strong national response, and they appeared on *The Tonight Show with Jay Leno* in 2005.

Honorable Mention

Everclean deserves solemn praise for their debut CD *Sons of Provo* from the movie of the same name. Will Swenson, Danny Tarasevich and Kirby Heyborne—with a huge assist from Jenny Jordan Frogley—have created the first LDS-based music CD that actually allows us to laugh at ourselves. An added bonus is that the music is top-notch and danceable. (Of course, I don't think the song "Sweet Spirit" is going to replace "Saturday's Warrior" as the final song at stake dances anytime soon.) The only question is whether this is a one-time project, or will Everclean be "putting their shoulders to the funk" in the future?

Top 5 LDS-based Male Recording Artists

1. **Michael McLean**
   Michael is a giant in the LDS market in terms of longevity, quality and creativity. He is a performer, composer, songwriter, producer and director, with a long list of accomplishments. Michael has written music and lyrics for 21 albums, most of which have been released by Deseret Book. They include best-selling classics such as *You're Not Alone, Celebrating the Light, A New Kind of Love Song, One Heart in the Right Place*, and the perennial favorite *The Forgotten Carols*. For more than a decade, Michael has performed *The Forgotten Carols* to sold-out audiences throughout the western United States during the Christmas season. Earlier in his career, Michael was the writer, producer and director of the films *Mr. Krueger's Christmas* and *Nora's Christmas Gift*. He has also played a key role in the creation and production of other well-known LDS-based films such as *Our Heavenly Father's Plan, Together Forever, A Labor of Love, What Is Real?* and *The Prodigal Son*. Michael also has two "best of" compilation CDs of his most-beloved songs.

2. **Kenneth Cope**
   Kenneth is best known for his original concept albums like *Greater Than Us All, Women at the Well*, and *Joseph Smith: The Seer*. He has won a variety of awards and is continually at the top of the LDS sales charts. His latest projects, *Hear My Praise* and *Face to Face*, break new ground in the LDS market. The CDs include his own original songs, along with his versions of some of the best-loved songs from other contemporary Christian artists. He is also a contributor to the *Son of Man* project that combines his music with the writing of Susan Easton Black and the art of Liz Lemon Swindle to tell the story of the Savior's life.

3. Lex de Azevedo

Lex is a true legend in the LDS recording industry who laid the groundwork for every LDS musician. He composed the popular musicals *Saturday's Warrior* and *My Turn on Earth*. With several other LDS-related projects over the years, such as the songs on the *Living Scriptures* videos, he has left his mark on the entire LDS entertainment industry. His six-CD set of instrumental arrangements entitled *Mormon Hymn Classics* is outstanding. His most recent project, *Gloria*, celebrates the Savior's life.

4. Kurt Bestor

Kurt's amazing instrumental arrangements have touched the lives of millions of listeners. His credits include more than 30 film scores and more than 40 themes for national TV programs and commercials Kurt is also renowned for his annual Christmas-themed performances and related CDs.

5. Steven Kapp Perry

Steven's albums in the late 1980s were just right for those not too intrigued by the big-hair heavy-metal bands or the mopey British popstars. His songs were filled with an upbeat cheerfulness that also taught gospel truths. Steven is still making music, and he is currently the host of Salt Lake radio station FM100's program *Soft Sunday Sounds*.

Honorable Mention

Bryce Neubert has long been one of the most popular LDS singers and songwriters in the industry. He is known for his exceptional tenor voice and easy-listening ballads that touch each listener with their spiritual poignancy.

Shane Jackman has already scaled the heights of the national folk music scene, but he has now turned to the LDS market with some great CDs. In 2005 he released the CD *Sanctuary*.

Top 5 LDS-based Female Recording Artists

1. **Janice Kapp Perry**
   She has written so many wonderful, inspiring faith-based songs that it is hard to keep count. The vast majority of the most-beloved songs both for Primary and for adults written since the 1970s have come from her. Even a list of her most popular songs don't quite touch the surface of her work, but here are just a few gems—*I'm Trying to Be Like Jesus, In the Hollow of Thy Hand, Love is Spoken Here, I Love to See the Temple, We'll Bring the World His Truth*, and so on. She is truly an inspired musician who remains genuinely humble about her accomplishments. She received the Lifetime Achievement Award from the Faith Centered Music Association in 2001.

2. **Julie de Azevedo**
   Most members of the Church first heard Julie's voice on recordings produced by her father, Lex de Azevedo. Her amazing voice stood out among the many other artists, both in tone and emotion. She then embarked on her solo career in 1988, and her CDs are known for their glimpses into everyday life. She now has seven solo albums, and her songs continue to grow in depth and quality. She has won several Pearl Awards, and her projects have been featured in films and television, and on the radio.

3. **Hillary Weeks**
   Hillary has been a top name in the LDS market for several years. Her CDs *He Hears Me* and *Lead Me Home* are among the biggest sellers in the industry. She has earned Pearl Awards for Songwriter of the Year, Female Vocalist of the Year, and Inspirational Album of the Year. She often participates in the *Time Out for Women* events that reach thousands of fans.

4. Cherie Call

Cherie is a talented singer and songwriter who is quickly gaining a large fanbase. Her songs, which are mostly ballads with a folk music flare, are applicable to everyone, yet are easily adapted to the life of each listener. Young women in particular seem to gravitate to her lyrics and melodies. Cherie graduated from BYU in 1997. She began recording several self-released albums, before joining Shadow Mountain. Her latest release is the best-selling CD *Beneath These Stars*. She has also been featured on the film soundtracks of *God's Army* and *Brigham City*. Cherie has been a regularly invited performer at Nashville's famous Blue Bird Café, and was honored with a Pearl Award for Female Recording Artist.

5. Maren Ord

This native of Canada has just released her second CD, *Not Today*, and she is one of the first LDS-based female recording artist to get substantial airplay on non-LDS stations. Maren is well-known by radio listeners in Canada, where her first CD, *Waiting*, was a major hit. She toured with Lillith Fair and was nominated for a Juno Award as "Best New Artist." Her song "Everyday" was included on *The Singles Ward* soundtrack and the video was included on the film's DVD.

Honorable Mention

Jenny Phillips is an extremely versatile songwriter and performer whose CDs tend to follow an overall theme, such as the popular *Parables* and *Journey Toward Zion*. She also performs dozens of firesides and concerts each year.

Jenny Oaks Baker takes the violin to a new spiritual level. She is one of America's most accomplished classical violinists. Her five CDs are inspiring and soothing, and her live performances are equally as powerful.

Top 5 LDS Artists/Illustrators

1. **Greg Olsen**
   Greg's artwork focuses predominately on the Savior and children. Born and raised in rural Idaho by parents who were also artists, Greg has honed his talents to emerge as one of the world's top artists. His oil paintings range from delicate, life-like portraits to fun, whimsical paintings as if seen through the eyes of a child. His works have been exhibited in prominent art galleries throughout the West and in major one-man shows. Greg's paintings are included in many corporate collections. Framed prints of his religious artwork sell very well to the general public and adorn the walls of many LDS homes.

2. **Del Parson**
   Del's most-recognized painting is his portrait of the Savior in a red robe. It was commissioned by the Church and was used for many years as part of the missionary discussions, and thus has been seen by millions of people. Del paints religious subjects to give others a sense of hope and share with them his love of life and its beauty. He has created a varied collection of paintings featuring scenes from the Savior's life. His paintings have received numerous regional and national awards.

3. **James Christensen**
   James is best-known for his fantasy themes. He taught art for more than 20 years, finishing his career at BYU in the late 1990s. He has been commissioned by numerous media companies to create artwork for their publications, such as Time/Life Books and Omni. James has won all the professional art honors the World Science Fiction Convention bestows. He has published three books, with many of his works appearing in many more. He was inducted into the U.S. Art magazine's Hall of Fame. He and his wife, Carole, co-chair the Mormon Arts Foundation.

4. Liz Lemon Swindle

Liz lets her abiding faith shine brightly through her art. She first established herself professionally as a wildlife painter at shows across the United States, before focusing on faith-based themes. Her dramatic *Son of Man* series has gained much recognition, and she is now regarded as one of the country's leading religious artists. Over the next several years, she will document the human events in the life of Christ through 50 unique paintings.

5. Simon Dewey

Simon didn't enter the world of LDS artwork until 1999, but his beautiful prints that mostly focus on the Savior's life soon became bestsellers. Simon is the only son of a London bus driver, and he left school at age 17 to pursue his artistic dreams. He later studied at a London art college before launching his career.

Honorable Mention

Ben Sowards is quickly establishing a strong reputation for vivid paintings that convey a story. He has already collaborated on several books, such as *The Christmas Oranges* and stories by Elder Thomas S. Monson and Elder Dieter F. Uchtdorf.

Brian Crane is the creative mind behind the *Pickles* comic strip that is syndicated in newspapers across the country.

Rhett Murray is known for a variety of award-winning artwork, particularly landscapes, but his religious artwork is rapidly gaining attention. His oil paintings having appeared in many art shows and on the covers of several LDS-based books.

Brett Helquist is an illustrator best known for his drawings in the children's books *A Series of Unfortunate Events*. Helquist earned a bachelor's degree in Fine Arts from BYU, and he currently lives in New York City.

Top 5 LDS-based Novelists

1. **Gerald Lund**
   By writing the landmark nine-volume series *The Work and the Glory*, Gerald would likely have earned this top spot for that effort alone. But he has written several other influential books, including the three-volume series *The Kingdom and the Crown* that follows a family living near Jerusalem at the time of the Savior. His earlier works are also highly regarded, with his 1983 novel *The Alliance* introducing many people to LDS fiction for the first time. He is also known for *The Coming of the Lord*, a doctrinal classic about the signs of the times and the last days. Gerald is now Elder Gerald N. Lund of the First Quorum of the Seventy and has currently put any future books on hold.

2. **Dean Hughes**
   Dean has been a prolific writer for many years, but his five-volume historical series *Children of the Promise*, centered around the fictional Thomas family's struggles during World War II and its aftermath, catapulted him to greater prominence. Dean then topped that with another five-volume series entitled *Hearts of the Children* that continued to follow the family through the 1960s and 1970s. Dean's early LDS novels, such as *Hooper Haller* and *Jenny Haller*, were also influential as the LDS fiction market began to develop in the early 1980s.

3. **Anita Stansfield**
   Anita is the LDS market's top-selling romance novelist, with sales of more than 500,000 copies of her thirty titles—and counting. Her latest novel, *Timeless Waltz*, is another strong seller. Her books are generally grouped into a particular series, such as the *Trevor Family Saga* or the *Gables of Legacy* series. Anita recently formed Crosswalk Books to publish her novels in *The Buchanan Saga* series.

ENTERTAINMENT

4. Chris Heimerdinger

Chris is best-known for his *Tennis Shoes Adventure Series* that follows friends Garth Plimpton, Jim Hawkins and their families as they time-travel to various times and locations in history. The novels opened up a whole new realm of LDS fiction, particularly to teen readers. The books also expanded the readers' imaginations, allowing them to better visualize how it would be to live in Book of Mormon and Bible times. Chris has also written several other books and is currently producing a movie based on his novel *Passage to Zarahemla*.

5. Rachel Ann Nunes

Rachel has written more than 20 romantic women's novels, and she is still going strong with a new series revolving around the fictional Huntington family. Her *Ariana* series is still a popular seller, along with her recently re-issued *Love* series, an adventure trilogy. Her award-winning picture book *Daughter of a King* and the follow-up *The Secret of the King* have also been big hits.

Honorable Mention

Ron Carter has completed nine volumes of his epic series *Prelude to Glory* that puts readers in the midst of the American Revolution. Ron has also written historical mystery novels.

Jennie Hansen has risen to prominence for her romantic adventure novels. She is producing an average of two novels a year, which keep her growing legion of fans happy.

Jeff Call is already one of the best LDS novelists, although he has only written three novels. His first novel, *Mormonville*, which follows an East Coast reporter as he settles undercover into a small Utah town to "expose" the Mormons, is already a classic that has sold thousands of copies. Jeff is a reporter himself, covering BYU sports for the *Deseret Morning News*.

Top 5 Nationally Published LDS Novelists

1. **Orson Scott Card**
   This prolific author has produced bestsellers in many categories. His novel *Ender's Game* has remained among the most popular science fiction novels ever since its debut in 1985. He has also branched out into contemporary fiction, such as the popular novels *Lost Boys*, *Treasure Box* and *Enchantment*. Some of his novels have religious themes, and LDS readers can easily spot the *Book of Mormon's* influence in his *Homecoming* series and the parallel to Joseph Smith's life in his *Alvin Maker* saga. He has also published several novels based on women in the Old Testament. He has had a busy career as a nonfiction writer, and he also was the screenwriter for the first *Living Scriptures* videos that were produced in the 1980s. He continues to produce outstanding stories at a rapid pace.

2. **Richard Paul Evans**
   Richard was working as an advertising executive in Utah when he wrote a Christmas story for his children entitled *The Christmas Box*. He tried to get it published, but only received rejections. In 1993 he decided to publish it himself and distribute it to local stores. Sales began to take off, and the rights were purchased by Simon & Schuster. The book became a phenomenon in 1995, becoming the first book to simultaneously reach the top position on the *New York Times* bestseller list for both the paperback and hardcover editions. That same year, the book was made into a television movie of the same title. Since that time, Richard has written a number of successful books with Christian themes and family values. He has also founded "The Christmas Box House International" charity to help neglected or abused children. His latest book is *The Sunflower*.

3. Dave Wolverton

Dave is a science-fiction author who has written several successful *Star Wars* novels. He also goes under the pseudonym David Farland for his fantasy works. His career began in 1987 when he won the top award in the L. Ron Hubbard "Writers of the Future" contest. He has been nominated for a Nebula Award and also for a Hugo Award. His latest novel is entitled *Of Mice and Magic*.

4. Anne Perry

Anne grew up in England, but lived for several years in the United States, where she joined the LDS Church. Her first novel was published in 1979. Her works generally fall into one of several categories of genre fiction, including historical mystery novels and fantasy. She has published nearly 50 novels and several collections of short stories. She now lives in Scotland.

5. Brenda Novak

Brenda writes romance from her home in Sacramento, California. Since first being published in 1998, she has sold 21 books to Harlequin. Brenda is a two-time Golden Heart finalist. Many of her titles have been designated a Romantic Times "Top Pick" and have gone on to place in contests such as the National Reader's Choice, the Bookseller's Best, The Write Touch Reader's Award, the Award of Excellence, and the Beacon Award for Published Authors.

Honorable Mention

Lee Nelson has written more than 30 books in the past three decades. His highly acclaimed *Storm Testament* historical novels put readers right in the middle of the Old American West with people such as Butch Cassidy and Indian chief Walkara. With the blessing of the Mark Twain Foundation, he completed Twain's unfinished novel *Huck & Tom Among the Indians* in 2003.

Top 5 LDS Actors

1. **Rick Schroder**
   Rick has been an actor for most of his life, and is a recent convert to the LDS Church. He debuted in the 1979 movie *The Champ*. He became well-known as the star of the television series *Silver Spoons* for several seasons. Following the end of that series, his career got a boost starring in the Western miniseries *Lonesome Dove* and its sequel, *Return to Lonesome Dove*. He also was a regular in the TV drama *NYPD Blue* and is currently starring in the TV series *Strong Medicine*. Rick recently branched out by directing and appearing in the music video for "Whiskey Lullaby," a hit song by country star Brad Paisley. For his work on this emotion-filled video, Rick was named Director of the Year at the 2005 CMT Video Music Awards.

2. **Matthew Modine**
   Matthew grew up in California as the youngest of seven children in a tight-knit LDS family. He has been in the acting business for nearly three decades, appearing in more than 50 movies and TV programs. His most-notable performances include roles in several big-budget films, such as *Full Metal Jacket*, *Memphis Belle*, *Married to the Mob*, *Any Given Sunday*, and *Notting Hill*. Matthew earned Golden Globe and Emmy Award nominations for his work in the TV drama *And The Band Played On*.

3. **Gordon Jump**
   Gordon is easily recognized by most Americans as the "Maytag Repairman." He played this role in commercials for Maytag brand appliances for many years. Gordon appeared in several TV productions, but his most prominent TV role was as the endearing but somewhat clueless radio station manager Arthur "Big Guy" Carlson in the 1970s TV series *WKRP in Cincinnati*. Gordon passed away in 2003.

ENTERTAINMENT

4. Billy Barty

Billy was born in Millsboro, Pennsylvania and later joined the LDS Church. He was one of the most famous actors of the 20th century with dwarfism, having prominent roles in popular movies such as *Foul Play*, *The Lord of the Rings* (1978 version), *Under the Rainbow*, *Masters of the Universe*, *Willow* and *UHF*. Billy was known for his quick wit, boundless energy, and enthusiasm for any productions in which he appeared. He was a noted activist for the promotion of rights for others with dwarfism, founding the Little People of America. Billy passed away in 2000.

5. Corbin Allred

Corbin has appeared in a variety of TV shows and movies. He was the star of the 2003 award-winning movie *Saints and Soldiers*, and starred in the 1990s television series *Teen Angel* before taking time off from acting to serve a mission to Australia. He currently has several movies in the works.

Honorable Mention

Dan Blocker is best remembered for his role as the husky, jovial brother "Hoss" Cartwright in the TV western *Bonanza*. His career was cut short when he died suddenly following routine gall bladder surgery in Los Angeles in 1972.

Jon Heder charmed the world in 2004 as the title character in the film *Napoleon Dynamite*, and he has continued his acting career in other films. **Aaron Ruell** certainly deserves notice for his memorable role as Napoleon's brother Kip, whose singing performance at his own wedding is unforgettable.

Kirby Heyborne and **Will Swenson** are definitely at the top of the list of actors making names for themselves in the LDS film industry. Both actors have already given several strong performances, with more surely on the way.

Top 5 LDS Actresses

1. **Eliza Dushku**
   Eliza has appeared in several big-budget movies such as *Bring It On* and *Wrong Turn*. She is also well-known for her acting on television, such as her recurring appearances as Faith on the TV series *Buffy the Vampire Slayer* and the show's spin-off *Angel*. She also starred in the TV series *Tru Calling*. She was born in Massachusetts, and raised in the LDS Church. Her acting career began to take off at age 12. Eliza stays close to her family and participates in events that benefit the Campaign for Tobacco-Free Kids. Now in her mid-20s with more than a dozen films to her credit, she is one of Hollywood's top actresses, equally adept at TV or movie roles.

2. **Keri Russell**
   Keri has firmly established herself as a talented actress. She has had a steady amount of acting opportunities ever since she was a regular on *The Micky Mouse Club* from 1991 to 1993. Soon after, she appeared as the babysitter in the Disney movie *Honey, I Blew Up the Kid*. Her breakout role came in 1998 as the title character in the network TV series *Felicity* that ran for several years. In 2005 she returned to television with an appearance in the Hallmark TV movie *Magic of Ordinary Days*. She has a role in the upcoming movie *Mission Impossible* 3 with Tom Cruise.

3. **Kelly Packard**
   Kelly began her career on the teen TV sitcom *California Dreams*. She later earned a regular role on *Baywatch*, one of the most popular TV shows in the world. Following that role, she served as a co-host on the TV series *Ripley's Believe It or Not* with Dean Cain. She most recently hosted the TV reality-remodeling series *House Wars*. She and her husband became the proud parents of a daughter in 2004.

ENTERTAINMENT   47

4. Katherine Heigl

Katherine is best known for her roles on the TV sci-fi series *Roswell* and in the TV medical drama *Grey's Anatomy*. She also had a major role in the film *The Ringer*. She has been steadily working in films for more than a decade, such as playing the older sister in the Disney Channel movie *Wish Upon a Star*, which was filmed in Utah. Among many other projects, she recently appeared to strong reviews in the Hallmark Channel movie *Love Falls Softly* and its sequel *Love's Enduring Promise*.

5. Jacque Grey

Jacque is best-known to LDS audiences as Sister Fronk in the movie *God's Army*, and as Miss Brigham in *Brigham City*. She also played Nephi's wife in *The Book of Mormon Movie*. But before she started acting in LDS-related works, she had a role in the movie *Drive Me Crazy* with Melissa Joan Hart, and appearances in the TV shows *Touched by an Angel* and *Promised Land*.

Honorable Mention

Loretta Young was a leading lady of the 1930s and 1940s and later hosted her own TV show. She was the first actress to win both an Oscar and an Emmy. She passed away in 2000.

Marie Osmond is definitely talented in many areas, and she is a household name across the world. This is in part due to the dozens of TV appearances she has made, in addition to being on *The Donny & Marie Show* in the 1970s and co-hosting a talk show with her brother Donny in recent years.

Sarah Schaub is best known as the teenage daughter Dinah Greene in the 1990s TV series *Promised Land*. Some of her other television credits include appearances on *One West Waikiki* and *Nothing Lasts Forever*. She also had a role in the miniseries *The Stand* and has had parts in several movies.

Top 5 LDS-related Television Moments

1. **The 2002 Winter Olympics**
   As the world descended on Salt Lake City for the 2002 Winter Olympics, some Utahns were a bit nervous about possible negative exposure that could result. But large portions of both the Opening and Closing ceremonies were devoted to Utah's pioneer heritage, and seemingly every visitor had only glowing things to say about Salt Lake, with comments ranging from the friendly people to the clean streets. NBC devoted several special segments to Church-related topics during the two-week event, and Temple Square seemingly got as much airtime as some of the events did. Overall, the Church and Utah came across very well to the more than one billion people who watched the Olympics.

2. **President Gordon B. Hinckley on 60 Minutes**
   When President Gordon B. Hinckley agreed to appear on the CBS new program *60 Minutes* shortly after becoming the Church's 15th president, the TV show's producers were stunned. They had tried for years to get an LDS Church president to appear, and now this new president readily agreed to an interview, saying he had nothing to hide. The interview went smoothly, and President Hinckley has since appeared again on *60 Minutes*, as well as shows such as *Larry King Live*. These interviews have helped clarify the Church's beliefs to the nation.

4. **Sharlene Wells winning the Miss America title**
   As the 1984 Miss America pageant entered its final hour, Miss Utah Sharlene Wells was among the finalists. Word quickly spread across Mormondom, and when the beautiful, talented BYU student won later that night on national TV, millions of Mormons across America felt like they had won, too.

ENTERTAINMENT 49

4. The Donny & Marie Show

This TV variety hour was like an ongoing funhouse for Osmond fans across the nation during the late 1970s. Each week millions of viewers would tune in to watch their good friends Donny and Marie. What kind of crazy capers they were up to now? Was Marie still a little bit country? Were Donny's socks still purple? Of course! And we loved it, from the comedy spoofs of *Star Wars* and *Grease* to their weekly final phrase, "Good night, everybody!" The Osmonds brought in some of America's biggest entertainers to their Orem, Utah, studio to perform during the show's four-year run. Never has missionary work been so entertaining, or had such high TV ratings. If you are now between the ages of 35 and 50 and claim you didn't love the show, you're not being honest with yourself.

5. Tabernacle Choir singing to President Reagan

In the 1980 U.S. presidential election, Ronald Reagan defeated President Jimmy Carter to claim the White House. The Mormon Tabernacle Choir was invited to be a part of the inauguration festivities by singing on a float during the inaugural parade. They would sing to the president as they passed his review stand. As the choir's float neared President Reagan, they burst into one of his favorite songs, "The Battle Hymn of the Republic." The new president was visibly touched by the music as he smiled, waved to the choir and wiped away a tear. The scene showed Reagan's sensitive, emotional side to millions of Americans for the first time, courtesy of the Mormon Tabernacle Choir.

Honorable mention

While not directly an LDS-related event, the TV miniseries *Roots*—based on Alex Haley's book about his ancestors—was a national sensation in the mid-1970s. It sparked great interest in family history research. Alex visited Salt Lake and was familiar with the Church's genealogy database. He passed away in 1992.

Top 5 LDS Reality TV Celebrities

1. **Ken Jennings**
   Ken became a living legend when he racked up 74 consecutive wins on the game show *Jeopardy* in 2004 for a total winnings of $2,522,700. He later won another $500,000 by finishing second in the show's Ultimate Tournament of Champions. Most of Ken's victories during his amazing win streak were by large margins, and only an incorrect answer in the Final Jeopardy portion of his 75th game prevented his streak from continuing. His record run boosted the ratings of the game show by 62 percent, drawing back viewers who hadn't watched the show in years. His streak also became a daily feature in newspapers across the country. Ken served a mission in Spain from 1993 to 1995 and was a member of the BYU College Bowl team in the 1990s.

2. **Carmen Rasmusen**
   Carmen caught everyone's attention on the second season of *American Idol* in early 2003 as the pretty blonde who actually dressed modestly. She hardly received any airtime during the show's preliminary rounds, but as the judges were making their "wildcard" selections, Carmen was chosen by judge Simon Cowell to continue on as one of the finalists. She performed on the show for the next several weeks, eventually finishing in the top six. She spent the summer on tour with the other *American Idol* finalists before spending a year at BYU. She appeared in the film *Pride and Prejudice* in 2003 and released her first music CD in 2004. The single "Photograph" has gained critical acclaim, even being named by *Billboard Magazine* editor Fred Bronson as one of his 10 favorite songs of 2004. Carmen recently married Brad Herbert in the Bountiful Utah Temple, and she is currently pursuing her country music career in Nashville, Tennessee.

ENTERTAINMENT

3. Neleh Dennis

Neleh appeared in 2002 on the fourth season of the reality TV series *Survivor*. She is from Layton, Utah and was only 21 at the time. She played the game very well and was one of the show's most likable contestants. She even took her scriptures as her luxury item. She reached the "Final Two" and came one vote short of winning the $1 million prize. But she left her mark on America, turning "Oh my heck!" into a national catchphrase. Following her stint on *Survivor*, Neleh was employed briefly by KUTV in Salt Lake City as a reporter for the morning show. She left the show in the summer of 2003 following her marriage to Kris Nielsen.

4. Shawn Nelson

Shawn was the winner of *The Rebel Billionaire*, in which he traveled around the world with other contestants and re-enacted crazy stunts that Richard Branson, an actual rebel billionaire, had performed in his lifetime. As the winner, Nelson received $1 million and a three-month position as the president of Branson's company Virgin Worldwide. Shawn has since returned to his job in Utah as CEO and president of LoveSac.

5. Jon Peter Lewis

JPL, as he was known during the third season of *American Idol*, became a finalist after performing the upbeat Elvis Presley song "A Little Less Conversation" while dancing all over the stage. JPL finished the season in eighth place. Prior to *American Idol*, he attended BYU-Idaho and served a mission to Spain. He resides in Los Angeles, where he continues his career in music.

Honorable Mention:

Ryan Benson was the winner in January 2005 of television's *The Biggest Loser*, a reality weight-loss show. He dropped from 330 pounds to 208 pounds during the course of the show.

Top 5 LDS-themed Highest-grossing Films (as of Dec. 31, 2005)

1. **The Other Side of Heaven ($4,720,000)**
   This retelling of Elder John H. Groberg's mission to Tonga was in theaters for nearly a full year and really picked up steam after it was picked up by Disney. As with all of the movies listed here, it has also sold well as a DVD through the LDS bookstores.

2. **The Work and the Glory ($3,347,000)**
   The film version of Elder Gerald Lund's first volume in the *The Work and the Glory* fiction series did quite well at the box office. It had a larger budget than any previous LDS film, and it was clearly the best LDS film yet in terms of cinematography.

3. **God's Army ($2,637,000)**
   This film is considered the first of the current wave of LDS-themed movies, and still ranks as one of the best. Richard Dutcher, a 1988 BYU film graduate, wrote, directed and starred in this film about Mormon missionaries in Los Angeles. The film didn't shy away from some of the horseplay and pranks missionaries inflict on each other. Some viewers who hadn't served missions felt the film irreverently overplayed that aspect of missionary life, while those who had actually served missions felt that the director got it just right. The whole production was completed on a $300,000 budget.

4. **The Work and the Glory: American Zion ($2,000,000)**
   This follow-up to *The Work and the Glory* is more exciting than the first movie, but hasn't quite matched it at the box office. It was still in some theaters at the end of 2005.

5. The Legend of Johnny Lingo - $1,690,000

This film is loosely tied to the 1960s BYU classic *Johnny Lingo* and is a good movie for kids, but isn't directly an LDS film.

Honorable Mention

Napoleon Dynamite is the biggest Mormon movie to not be labeled that way. Of course, it is also likely the only major movie to have the main character wear a "Ricks College" T-shirt. Jared and Jerusha Hess co-wrote and directed the film, which was shot in Preston, Idaho. They met while attending BYU's film school, and the film was produced and edited by classmate Jeremy Coon. Jared and Jerusha both graduated from BYU in late 2003. The film had a production budget of $400,000. The film was shown at the 2004 Sundance Film Festival and the distribution rights were purchased by Fox Searchlight. It turned out to be a wise move. Domestic ticket sales at U.S. theaters alone stand at just under $45 million, with an additional $1.5 million overseas. The film's release on DVD has added millions to the coffers. Jon Heder, who played Napoleon, didn't get rich making the film, but it has opened the doors for other acting opportunities.

New York Doll is a documentary by LDS director Greg Whitely that premiered at the Sundance Film Festival to strong reviews. The film follows mild-mannered LDS convert Arthur Kane as he works at the Church's Los Angeles Family History Library. However, Kane was once "Killer" Kane of the influential 1970s band The New York Dolls. When British rock star Morrissey, a huge fan of the band, asks them to reunite for a concert, Kane nervously decides to participate. This is a unique look at an LDS convert's life, especially coming from a celebrity background.

Halestorm has made several popular LDS-based movies, with **The Singles Ward** their leading moneymaker at $1.25 million in ticket sales. The Halestorm movies sell very well on DVD.

Prominent People: Inventors, Businessmen, and Political Leaders

The Church has always had bright men and women who invent new ways to do things. Some of these inventions have changed our way of life. Likewise, many LDS businessmen and political leaders have shaped the path of the nation and the world. As each year passes, the Church and its members are playing a bigger role in the world's future.

Top 5 LDS Inventors

1. Philo Farnsworth
Philo is known as the "Father of Television." He was 13 years old and living in Rigby, Idaho, when the idea of transmitted electronic images first came to him. By 1927 he had actually created such a gadget, and he and his research team continued to perfect his new invention though the 1930s. Televisions began to be sold commercially soon after World War II. Philo was involved in research in many other areas. He invented the first electron microscope and the first infant incubator. He was involved in the development of radar, peacetime uses of atomic energy, and the nuclear fusion process. At his death, Farnsworth held 300 U.S. and foreign patents. *Scientific American* magazine called him one of the ten greatest mathematicians of his time.

2. Robert. B. Ingebretsen
Robert was true pioneer in digital sound technology. In 1999, he received an Academy Award for his work that has changed each of our lives. He invented technology that translated analog sound into a digital format. This discovery that eventually led to the development of compact discs and DVDs.

3. John Moses Browning
John was the world's most famous firearms designer. He had 128 patents, and the guns that bear his name have marked every armed conflict from World War I through Desert Storm. Browning rifles and shotguns are considered some of the best hunting equipment in the world today.

4. Harvey Fletcher
Harvey was considered the father of stereophonic sound. He was born in Provo and was credited with more than 20 inventions in audio technology, including the first hearing aid.

PROMINENT PEOPLE

5. Nolan Bushnell

Nolan is the inventor of "Pong" and the Atari 2600 home videogame system. While attending Stanford University, he converted his daughter's room into a lab where he created "Computer Space," the first marketable video game. He soon realized the game was too difficult for the average consumer, so he dumbed it down and created "Pong" in 1972. It was also during this time that Nolan invented the hugely successful Atari 2600. He later sold Atari to Warner Communications, but retained ownership of his Chuck E. Cheese pizza parlors until the early 1980s.

Honorable Mention

Robert K. Jarvik invented the artificial heart. It was first implanted in a human patient, Barney Clark, in 1982.

William Hall invented the process of creating synthetic diamonds.

Alvino Rey invented the electric guitar, essentially paving the way for rock and roll.

Rose Marie Reid invented the first women's buttonless one-piece bathing suit, and the first photopermeable swimsuit that allowed full-body tanning without removing the suit.

Don Carlos Edwards blessed our lives by inventing the tasty concoction known as Fry Sauce. He created it by mixing ketchup with mayonnaise, pickle juice and a special blend of spices. It was first sold through his Arctic Circle restaurants.

A report on CNN in 2000 credited Mormons for creating the scrapbooking craze, which now takes place in nearly a quarter of all U.S. homes. The report didn't specify which Mormon gets the actual credit, but I would guess it was a Homemaking leader.

Top 5 Best-known LDS Businessmen

1. **James L. Sorenson, CEO of Sorenson Media**
   This quiet billionaire shuns the spotlight, but he has a history of making generous donations to the LDS Church, such as a $5 million donation to the Church's Perpetual Education Fund and more than $30 million for the restoration of the Nauvoo Illinois Temple. James has been a lifelong entrepreneur and made his first fortune selling medical devices. He now invests in digital technologies through his company Sorenson Media. He is listed by Forbes Magazine as among the word's richest people, currently worth $2.2 billion.

2. **Jon Huntsman, Sr., CEO of Huntsman Chemical**
   Through his determination and wise decisions, Jon has turned Huntsman Chemical Corporation into the world's largest privately held chemical company. The company manufactures basic products of nearly every variety, including plastics, footwear, paints and coatings, construction, technology, agriculture, and so on. His establishment of the Huntsman Cancer Center near the University of Utah has blessed many lives. Jon is also an author, having recently published the book *Winners Never Cheat*.

3. **J. Willard Marriott of Marriott Hotels**
   He developed the drive-in restaurant, and later expanded the business to include hotels. The Marriott hotel chain is known across the world for its quality and reliability in meeting the needs of its customers. He was a generous contributor to higher education, and the Marriott Center at BYU and the Marriott Library at the University of Utah bear his name. He passed away in 1986, but his son, J.W. Marriott, has continued to expand the company, which is now known as Marriott International.

4. Steven R. Covey of FranklinCovey

Steven founded the largest management and leadership development organization in the world, now known as FranklinCovey. He is the author of several books and is perhaps best known as the author of *The 7 Habits of Highly Effective People*, which was a long-time No. 1 bestseller. The book has sold more than 12 million copies in 32 languages and 75 countries throughout the world.

5. Hal Wing, Little Giant Ladders

Hal's perseverance and belief in his product has resulted in one of the fastest-growing companies in the world. Hal started as a one-person company in his garage, perfecting the prototype for his Little Giant ladder. Then he went on the road, selling it at trade shows and demonstrating why the ladder is considered the most sturdy and versatile one in the world. He founded Wing Enterprises to manufacture the ladder, and through a popular infomercial, the word about the product is getting out. The company's sales will reach at least $600 million in 2006.

Honorable Mention

The list of successful LDS businesspeople is truly astounding. This is by far the biggest group of possible candidates among the categories in this book, and new successes seem to emerge every year. Below are listed some of these many business leaders who continue to make a difference in the world.

J. Ralph Atkin, Skywest Airlines
Gene and Kristine Hughes, Nature's Sunshine Products
Steve Lund, CEO of NuSkin International
Larry H. Miller, Utah businessman, owner of the Utah Jazz
David Neeleman, CEO of JetBlue Airways
Ray Noorda, CEO of Novell
Kevin Rollins, CEO of Dell Computer Corporation

Top 5 Best-known LDS Political Leaders

1. Orrin Hatch

As a five-term senator from Utah, Orrin has built a strong legacy of public service in Washington, D.C. He was elected in 1976 and is running for a sixth term in 2006. He is the second-ranking Republican on the U.S. Senate Committee on Finance, where he serves on the Subcommittee on International Trade and several other subcommittees. He also serves on the Board of Directors for the United States Holocaust Memorial Museum. He also devotes his spare time to writing uplifting hymns, and he has collaborated with Janice Kapp Perry on a patriotic CD.

2. Mike Leavitt

Mike served as Utah's governor for eleven years and was president of the National Governors Association. In 2003, Mike was named by President George W. Bush as the Administrator of the Environmental Protection Agency (EPA). In 2004, President Bush asked him to serve as Secretary of the Department of Health and Human Services. He is the head of 66,000 employees who provide essential human services to all Americans in need.

3. Mitt Romney

Mitt is currently the governor of Massachusetts, but has announced he won't run again. Many political observers say he is testing the waters for a run at the U.S. presidency in 2008. He is the son of Michigan's former governor George W. Romney. Prior to winning the governorship, Mitt was best known for his role as the head of the Salt Lake Olympic Committee and making the 2002 Winter Olympics a triumphant success. In 1984, Mitt founded Bain Capital, one of the nation's most successful venture capital and investment companies.

4. Harry Reid

Harry is a U.S. senator for the state of Nevada. He was elected in 1986 and is currently serving his fourth term. He is the Democratic Leader in the Senate. He has developed a reputation as a consensus builder and a skillful legislator. Even his Republican colleagues praise his reasoned, balanced approach. He was born and raised in the little town of Searchlight, Nevada, and continues to be an advocate for working middle-class families.

5. Ezra Taft Benson

During the 1950s he served on President Dwight Eisenhower's cabinet as the Secretary of Agriculture. He also was serving as a member of the Quorum of the Twelve Apostles at the time and his young family was featured in national magazines, where they explained their beliefs and demonstrated "Family Night." When President Eisenhower left the Oval Office, Elder Benson returned to full-time Church service and became the 13th president of the LDS Church in 1985. He passed away in 1994.

Honorable Mention

Reed Smoot served in the U.S. Senate from 1903 to 1933, while also serving as an apostle. His contributions can't be underestimated in helping Utah and the Church from being treated unfairly in the first few years after Utah received statehood.

Other current LDS U.S. governors and senators are:
Jon Huntsman, Jr., Utah's governor, elected in 2004.
Bob Bennett, U.S. senator for Utah, elected in 1992.
Gordon Smith, U.S. senator for Oregon, elected in 1996.
Mike Crapo, U.S. senator for Idaho, elected in 1998.

Several members of the U.S. House of Representatives belong to the LDS Church.

Bibliography

Book resources

2006 *LDS Church Almanac*, Deseret Morning News, Salt Lake City, 2006.

Bronson, Fred. *The Billboard Book of Number 1 Hits*, Billboard Books, New York, 2003.

Whitburn, Joel. *The Billboard Book of Top 40 Hits*, Billboard Books, 1992.

Internet resources

Billboard.com
Boxofficemojo.com
BYUCougars.com
Deseretbook.com
Deseretnews.com
FamousMormons.net
Imdb.com
LDS.org
MeridianMagazine.com
MLB.com
NFL.com
NBA.com
PGA.com
UtahUtes.com
Wikipedia.org

Much of the information was gathered and summarized from the personal websites of many of the featured individuals.

About the Author

Chad Daybell lives in Springville, Utah, with his wife Tammy and their five children.

Chad is the author of 18 books, which include a variety of LDS-based non-fiction books such as *Baptism*, *The Aaronic Priesthood*, and *The Youth of Zion*. He also is the author of the award-winning fiction series *The Emma Trilogy* and the popular novel *Chasing Paradise*.

To learn more about Chad and to see a complete listing of his books, along with their descriptions, please visit his website at **www.cdaybell.com**.

Do you know of a category or person we may have overlooked?

If you have an LDS Top 5 category or person that you feel deserves inclusion in an upcoming edition of the book, please contact us at **top5@springcreekbooks.com**.

Also, we welcome any comments about the rankings or additional information about anyone included in the lists. If you are providing factual information, we ask that you provide a way to verify the information.